MAGGIE L. WALKER

MAGGIE L. WALKER

PIONEERING BANKER AND COMMUNITY LEADER

Candice Ransom

Twenty-First Century Books/Minneapolis

Acknowledgments: The author wishes to thank everyone at the Maggie L. Walker National Historic Site and the Richmond National Battlefield Park for giving me access to research materials, granting interviews, answering endless questions, and reviewing my manuscript, with special thanks to Celia "Miss Maggie" Suggs, who knows more about Maggie L. Walker than any living person. This book could not have happened without any of you.

Twenty-First Century Books
A division of Lerner Publishing Group, Inc.
241 First Avenue North
Minneapolis, MN 55401 U.S.A.

Website address: www.lernerbooks.com

Library of Congress Cataloging-in-Publication Data

Ransom, Candice F., 1952–
    Maggie L. Walker: pioneering banker and community leader / by Candice F. Ransom.
        p.   cm. — (Trailblazer biographies)
    Includes bibliographical references and index.
    ISBN 978–0–8225–6611–3 (lib. bdg. : alk. paper)
    1. Walker, Maggie Lena, 1867–1934—Juvenile literature. 2. African American women—Virginia—Richmond—Biography—Juvenile literature. 3. African Americans—Virginia—Richmond—Biography—Juvenile literature. 4. African American bankers—Virginia—Richmond—Biography—Juvenile literature. 5. African American businesspeople—Virginia—Richmond—Biography—Juvenile literature. 6. Richmond (Va.)—Biography—Juvenile literature. I. Title.
    F234.R553W353 2009
    305.48'8960730092—dc22 [B]   2007042906

Manufactured in the United States of America
1 2 3 4 5 6 – BP – 14 13 12 11 10 09

CONTENTS

CHAPTER ONE

FROM MANSION TO ALLEY

Nine-year-old Maggie tugged at her end of the laundry basket. She and her little brother, Johnnie, carried the heavy basket between them. If they were lucky, Maggie and Johnnie would receive a few pennies for delivering the clothes their mother had washed and ironed. But Johnnie was so busy gawking at the carriages and wagons on Grace Street in Richmond, Virginia, he often let the handle slide from his small fingers. Like most six-year-old boys, Johnnie was fascinated with wheels.

When they stopped again, it was in front of a mansion high on Church Hill at Twenty-third and Grace streets. The three and a half story house with its six white columns was a grand structure. Its terraced gardens commanded a view of the James River.

Across from the mansion was Saint John's Church, where, in 1775, Patrick Henry thundered his powerful speech. He urged colonists to take up arms against the British in what would become the Revolutionary War (1775–1783). Henry asked, "Is life so dear, is peace so sweet, as to be purchased at the price of chains and slavery? Forbid it, Almighty God. I know not what course others make take, but as for me, give me liberty or give me death!"

The mansion was the home of Elizabeth Van Lew. Miss Lizzie, as everyone in Richmond called her, was a nervous, birdlike woman. Some of the neighborhood kids were afraid of her. When Maggie knew her, Miss Lizzie was shunned by Richmond society. Even though Virginia was in the South, a Confederate state, Miss Lizzie was a spy for the North (the Union) in the Civil War (1861–1865).

During the war, Elizabeth Van Lew visited Union officers held captive in a nearby Confederate prison. She brought them medicine, food, and other necessities. She smuggled out messages in hollow-shelled eggs and books with pinpricked words that spelled out secret information. Dressed as a country woman and mumbling loudly to herself, she gave the impression of being crazy. She earned the nickname "Crazy Bet," coined by a newspaper in Boston, Massachusetts. It was the perfect cover for a spy.

Van Lew also hid Union soldiers in a secret room in her mansion. When the Confederates were taking horses for the army, Van Lew hid her last horse in the upstairs library, muffling the horse's hooves with a thick layer of straw. Van Lew used her freed black servants to pass secret messages. She sent one of her servants to work in the home of the Confederate president, Jefferson Davis. She also helped slaves escape to freedom.

Maggie gazed at the big brick house. "I was born *in* or *at* the Van Lew's mansion," Maggie Walker

Maggie Lena Walker was born in the Van Lew mansion *(above)* in Richmond, Virginia. Maggie's mother, a former slave, was employed by Elizabeth Van Lew.

reminisced in her 1925 diary. She had been four when she moved and had vague memories of living there.

No birth certificate states the date of Maggie's birth. Some records show she was born in 1864 or 1865. The 1900 census records Maggie's birth as July 1865. Maggie claimed she was born on July 15, 1867. Maggie was a popular name at the time, either by itself or as a nickname for Margaret. Sometimes African American girls, like Maggie, were named after a grandmother. Maggie may have been named after her grandmother, Margaret Draper.

Maggie's mother, Elizabeth Draper, was born in Powhatan County, west of Richmond. Eventually Elizabeth Draper came to the city. Though records show Elizabeth Van Lew both hired and bought slave women, she made no reference to hiring or buying Maggie's mother. Elizabeth Draper was freed before the Civil War, but she stayed on at the Van Lew mansion as a cook's helper.

Maggie's father was Eccles Cuthbert, a white journalist who wrote for the *New York Herald* and the *Richmond Dispatch*. Max, as he was called, was a snappy dresser with a long beard and a heavy Irish accent. No one knows where Elizabeth Draper and Cuthbert met, but it is possible that Cuthbert knew Elizabeth Van Lew. He may have been invited to a

Elizabeth Van Lew, photographed here in the late 1800s, was a southerner from Richmond, Virginia. She sympathized with Union troops during the Civil War.

gathering at her home, where he would have seen Maggie's mother. They never married.

It was illegal at that time for whites to marry African Americans in Virginia. Even freed slaves were not allowed to marry. In 1867 Virginia's General Assembly passed a law allowing marriages between black men and women.

Elizabeth Draper knew her daughter Maggie needed a father. She accepted an offer of marriage from William Mitchell, the mixed-race Van Lew butler. They were married in the First African Baptist Church (FABC) on May 27, 1868. Though Elizabeth gave her age as twenty and William claimed to be thirty, it is possible they were both younger. Slaves and

Maggie's mother, Elizabeth Draper *(left)*, married William Mitchell *(right)* in 1868.

free blacks were not always listed in census records.

The long Civil War had ended three years before. Richmond, the capital of the Confederacy, had fallen when Union troops marched into the city. Confederate general Robert E. Lee had surrendered his army to Union general Ulysses S. Grant at Appomattox Court House, Virginia, on April 9, 1865. A few days later, President Lincoln had been assassinated at Ford's Theatre, in Washington, D.C.

Although Lincoln had freed the slaves with his Emancipation Proclamation in 1863, slavery was outlawed by the Thirteenth Amendment to the Constitution in 1865 With the war over, the defeated South had to rebuild and cope with change. Union military forces occupied southern cities such as Richmond to keep order. Freed slaves streamed in from countryside plantations, looking for work. Richmond's streets were filled with wandering ex-slaves who needed jobs, homes, food, and clothing.

The southern states were under the control of the U.S. government while they were recovering from the war in this period, called Reconstruction. The United States also created an agency to deal with the problems faced by newly freed slaves. The Freedmen's Bureau helped them obtain necessities such as food, medicines, and farm tools. The bureau served as a protective agency, to defend slaves from former owners, who wanted to force them back to work. It also opened schools for African American children. Northerners, particularly women, came to the South to help African

Americans forge new lives. The women, called Yankee schoolmarms, were usually teachers.

After her mother's marriage, Maggie's new step-father decided to look for a better-paying position that offered opportunity for advancement. He was fortunate to find a job as a waiter at the fancy St. Charles Hotel. To be closer to his work, William moved his wife and daughter from the Van Lew mansion to one of two small wooden houses on College Alley, just off Broad Street.

In 1870 Maggie's brother John B. Mitchell was born. Maggie often had to watch her mischievous brother. Both Maggie and Johnnie were drawn to the action on the busy city streets.

William Mitchell moved his family into this small house on College Alley in Richmond. Maggie spent her childhood years in this house, located near Richmond's state capitol building.

Parades and marching bands passed by the capitol building, across Broad Street from Maggie's house. The city's many organizations and militias (citizen armies) hosted parades for all occasions. The sound of horns and drums sent a thrill up Maggie's spine. She loved the marchers' costumes and their precise steps. Across the alley and two blocks up from the Mitchell house, the First African Baptist Church often held revivals, concerts, festivals, and meetings. The whole world seemed to pass by Maggie Walker's doorstep!

The area Maggie lived in was one of the new voting districts created after the Civil War. It was called Jackson Ward. The ward's name probably came from former president Andrew Jackson, since several other precincts (districts) were named after former presidents such as Monroe, Jefferson, and Madison.

Some of the houses in the area dated back to 1790. The earliest citizens in the neighborhood hailed from Italy, Germany, and other European countries. Jackson Ward didn't become a predominantly (almost all) black neighborhood until after the war. Whites resided in the nicer homes on Grace Street, while blacks lived in small houses without yards near the Chesapeake and Orange railroad tracks. Near this area was Shockoe Bottom, once the site of Lumpkin's slave auction house.

In her travels along Broad Street, Maggie passed Bell's grocery, Jackson's store, Luckadoo's shoe shop, and Isham's barbershop. She paused outside of each business in case something interesting was happening inside.

Horse-drawn wagons hauling produce from outlying farms clip-clopped down Broad Street. Covered market carts, pulled by mules, carried dressed chickens and turkeys. Maggie ran after two-wheeled vegetable carts, hoping for a free sun-ripened tomato grown in Hanover County. An even better sight was the Italian organ grinder. He played lively tunes while his little monkey danced, sweeping off its tiny cap for pennies. Most tempting of all though was the circus. The lot where Robinson's Circus set up was near Maggie's house. Maggie and Johnnie stole away to Robinson's Circus to watch high-wire acrobats. Lewis, a black bareback rider, hopped on and off a running elk.

Maggie's family was happy and doing well when tragedy struck. One February night in 1876, William Mitchell did not come home from work. No one knew what had happened to him. Eight-year-old Maggie and her mother frantically asked neighbors if they had seen him.

After a five-day search by the authorities, William Mitchell's body was found in the James River. The coroner's official report stated suicide by drowning, but Maggie's mother did not believe it. She knew of no reason why he would kill himself. Elizabeth was certain her husband had been murdered, possibly while being robbed. She believed his body had been thrown in the river to cover up the crime.

While Maggie's family would never learn the truth, they had bigger problems. Even though William had earned a good salary and tips, the Mitchells had lived from payday to payday. They had no savings or insurance.

Maggie's family was suddenly poor. With two small children to support, Elizabeth Mitchell began washing clothes for white people. It was a job suitable for young widows, and it would allow her to stay home with Maggie and Johnnie. The children were put to work helping their mother.

"I worked all day and way into the night," Maggie later wrote. "Work—or starve—that was my mandate."

On Mondays, Maggie, Johnnie, and their mother collected clothes from the customers. At home Maggie and her mother built a fire under the big washtub outside. Maggie drew water from the well, poured it

After Maggie's stepfather died, her mother did laundry to make a living for her young family. Maggie helped out. This photograph, taken in 1887, shows what a typical day might have been like. Clothes were boiled in tubs of water over a fire *(left)* and then scrubbed clean on washboards *(right)*.

A young girl in 1900 scrubs clothes on a washboard, as Maggie would have done.

into the tub, and heated it. While the water heated, Elizabeth sorted clothes. Then she boiled them in the kettle. Maggie rubbed homemade lye soap into the clothes on a metal washboard until her knuckles were skinned raw. She helped wring the clothes by hand. After a rinse in more water, they were again wrung out. Then they were ready to be starched.

Maggie and her mother made starch from flour and water mixed with a little kerosene. They dipped the garments into the starch water. Then they pinned shirts, sheets, pants, and skirts to a line to dry. Dry clothes were dampened with water and rolled up until ironing day.

No matter how hot it was outside, Elizabeth used three irons. The three irons were heated on the stove, and two stayed hot there while she ironed with the third. The bottoms of the irons were coated with beeswax so they would glide smoothly across the fabric. Elizabeth was careful not to scorch women's delicate blouses. The work was backbreaking, but her family's income depended on her.

Elizabeth was not the only laundress in the city. At the time, Richmond employed 784 laundresses. All were African American women. Elizabeth Mitchell undoubtedly knew other laundresses. Possibly Elizabeth and other women shared their work, discussing problems in the community as they rubbed clothes on washboards or pumped water from the well. Maggie may have listened to them and learned about solving problems.

On Saturdays Maggie and her brother delivered the clean, fresh-smelling laundry to the customers. Other laundresses carried baskets on their heads as they made their deliveries. When Maggie was a little older, she did too. "I was not born with a silver spoon in my mouth, but with a laundry basket practically on my head," she said.

When Maggie and Johnnie made their rounds one Saturday, the children were each rewarded with a penny at the last house. Johnnie said he was going to buy candy at the corner market. Maggie looked thoughtfully at the coin in her palm.

CHAPTER TWO

MAGGIE MITCHELL'S ALLEY

"You, Maaaggie!" called Elizabeth Mitchell from the alley's entrance.

Maggie, aged nine, was sitting on the curb, watching a train. The tracks of the Richmond, Petersburg, and Potomac Railroad split Broad Street in the middle. As the cars rolled by, Maggie may have wondered about the passengers inside. Where were they going? Were they going to have an adventure?

"You, Maaaggie!" Her mother's voice carried up the alley as the last cars clattered past.

Maggie hurried home, down Maggie Mitchell's Alley. Her mother called her from the entrance of the alley so often that Maggie's friend and classmate Wendell Dabney renamed her street.

Maggie figured her mother wanted her to help with the laundry or to watch Johnnie. Impish and sweet faced, Johnnie Mitchell was forever dashing out of the alley. Their mother would yell at him to come back, but usually Maggie would be sent after her six-year-old brother.

In addition to her laundry job, Maggie's mother became a midwife, helping women in the area de-

Maggie helped to watch over her younger half brother, Johnnie Mitchell.

liver babies. She also took in boarders for a while. Not too long after William Mitchell's death, Maggie's uncle Frederick moved in with the family and stayed a few years. Her mother's younger brother, Ed, also came to live with the Mitchells. Both men worked as laborers. They probably contributed to the household income. During the early 1870s, Richmond's African American population still struggled to make ends meet. Extended families often lived together to share rent and other expenses.

But Elizabeth could not count on her brothers' support forever. So she scrubbed and ironed from dawn till dark, in the freezing cold and sweltering heat. She wanted better for her children, especially Maggie.

Elizabeth didn't want her daughter to have to bend over a hot tub stirring bedsheets or ironing shirts until her back ached like a bad tooth. Education was the key to a better life, Elizabeth knew. She could neither read nor write. But Maggie would learn.

In mid-October 1872, Maggie started first grade at the Old Lancaster School at the bottom of the hill. This school, Richmond's first public school, had been closed. The school board reopened it as a primary school for African American children. Following the war, when free black schools were set up, the Yankee schoolmarms taught in most of them. But at Old Lancaster, the teachers were southern white women.

Freedmen's schools serving only African American children opened throughout the South after the Civil War ended in 1865. This school is in North Carolina. Maggie attended a similar school in Richmond.

Though Maggie's school was renamed the Valley School, most people still referred to it as Old Lancaster. The building had three large rooms on each of the two floors. Across from the school was the jail. Shortly after the Civil War, vagrancy laws were passed to keep the homeless off the streets. Many African American women and men without jobs or homes were jailed for vagrancy. Maggie and her friend Wendell often heard prisoners shouting at one another or singing spirituals such as "Roll, Jordan, Roll" and "Steal Away."

Maggie learned to read and write, using the Bible and McGuffey's Readers, a reading textbook series. She had heard that reading and writing were like riding the wind—a person could go anywhere.

She also studied arithmetic, map drawing, geography, spelling, and history. She was a good student and was promoted regularly to each grade.

The First African Baptist Church, where her parents were married, was across the street and up the block from her house. It was a source of never-ending fascination to Maggie. Sitting on the curb, she watched people dressed in their best outfits walk to Sunday services. But the church wasn't interesting only on Sundays. The impressive brick structure buzzed with events all the time. It was the center of the African American community.

One Sunday when Maggie was ten, she was outside on College Alley, playing in her oldest clothes. A gentleman from the church noticed her, crossed the street, and came toward her. He asked her what her name was and where she lived. She responded firmly that she was Maggie Lena Mitchell and she lived on College Alley. Next, the man asked her about her parents. Maggie replied that her mother did washing and ironing for other people and her father was dead.

The man was Deacon William White. He asked Maggie if she would like to play with other children in the church. Maggie said yes, and the man took her into the church.

The inside of the great church filled her with awe. The sanctuary, with its polished pews and stained glass windows, took her breath away. She had never seen anything so beautiful.

In the basement, she was introduced to the other children. Maggie listened to Bible stories and played games. She liked the other children and the teacher. Sunday school was a lot like regular school. Maggie learned that adults joined FABC's Sunday school to learn to read.

The next Sunday, Maggie was neatly dressed and waiting outside the church. No one in the Mitchell home attended Sunday school, but on her own, Maggie decided she would go.

Soon Maggie was attending the services as well. Sitting in the beautiful sanctuary, she felt a strong sense of community and a sense of belonging to this place. She was no longer little Maggie Lena whiling away the time playing in the dirt or scrubbing clothes on the washboard. The simple gesture of Deacon White offering his hand opened her eyes to the wider world beyond College Alley.

Maggie found a loving community at the nearby First African Baptist Church *(above)*. *S*he would spend much of her spare time there learning about the Bible, attending Sunday school, and spending time with other children. A new church building was built on this site in 1876.

In the summer of 1878, Maggie Lena Mitchell was baptized as a member of the First African Baptist Church. Religious fervor swept Richmond and the rest of the country that summer during what was called the Great Revival. The Reverend James H. Holmes, the minister who had married Maggie's mother and William Mitchell, baptized hundreds of new members the last week of May and into June.

Maggie was third on the list on that special day. She wore a new white robe and walked with dignity with the other children down to the James River.

Birds sang in the treetops, lending sweet music to the joyful occasion.

The Reverend Holmes led Maggie into the shallow water and held her as he dipped her back into the river. Filled with a joy she'd never experienced before, Maggie waded out of the river and up the bank. She was a new person.

Years later, she reflected on the importance of Jackson Ward in her life, "I was reared in the first alley just off Broad Street, there; taught Sunday School here, and day school down in the valley just at the foot of the hill. Every foot of ground in this historic and sacred lot and all around this neighborhood

Hundreds of parishioners and townspeople, including Maggie, gathered to join and witness a mass baptism that took place on the banks of the James River in Richmond during the the Great Revival in 1878. This engraving by W. L. Sheppard appeared in *Frank Leslie's Illustrated Newspaper* in 1878.

is precious to me, for I have roamed and romped over it all in my happy, thoughtless, childhood days."

After graduating from primary school, Maggie attended the Navy Hill secondary school for two years. Maggie was fortunate to go to Navy Hill, the only school in the city with an African American teaching staff. Miss Lizzie Knowles, the white principal, was a northern missionary (a religious or humanitarian aid worker). She wore her gray braids like a crown, giving her a saintly appearance. Even so, she guided faculty and students with a firm but fair hand. In those two years, Maggie learned about saving money, serving the community and, most important, being proud of her race.

Much later, Maggie spoke fondly of the educators who "guided our childish feet, trained our restless hands, and created within our youthful souls . . . an undying ambition to be something, and to do something . . . to lift ourselves and our people from the degradation of innocence and ignorance and poverty to competence, culture, and respectability."

School and church expanded Maggie's world. Though still young, she was moving beyond the wooden house on College Alley and into the community she hoped to serve.

CHAPTER THREE
SPEAKING OUT

At Navy Hill School, Maggie had learned the importance of racial pride, along with reading, writing, and arithmetic. She wanted to make a difference, so she decided to become a teacher and inspire African American children.

After two years at Navy Hill, Maggie went to high school. The high school was also a normal school. "Normal" meant that the school prepared students to teach. The school included junior, intermediate, and senior years. The normal department offered teacher training during the final year. Competing with students all over the city, Maggie took an exam to gain entrance into the school. She earned one of the forty openings.

The Freedmen's Bureau had opened the first Colored Normal School in Richmond in 1867. After being denied an education for so long, African American students filled the school. Two teachers taught sixty-five students. Soon the old building was too small. Skilled laborers from the community built a new structure on North Twelfth Street.

Maggie's courses were tough—United States and ancient history, penmanship, literature, writing, debating, arithmetic, algebra, physiology, physics, chemistry, geography, and astronomy. She studied hard because she wanted to be a teacher.

Miss Knowles, the principal from Navy Hill, had become principal at the normal school. The teachers were white, too, but not all were as dedicated as Miss Knowles. Some, such as the art and music teachers, were part-time. Others taught as though they believed the job was beneath them.

Maggie admired Miss Knowles, but she felt African American teachers would be better for the children because they understood the African American community. Even as a teenager, Maggie was thinking about how she might best help the people in Jackson Ward. Maggie regularly attended the Thursday night Sunday school practice meetings and other social events at the First African Baptist Church. As she blossomed into a confident young woman, aware of the world around her, she was still looking for other ways to serve.

When Maggie was fourteen and in her second year of normal school, she became a member of the Good Idea Council #16 of the Independent Order of the Sons and Daughters of St. Luke. The moment she was accepted, her life changed forever.

In the 1870s and 1880s, Richmond abounded with fraternal organizations. These groups began as secret societies in the days when it was illegal for slaves to start schools or meet in large groups.

Maggie attended the Colored Normal School *(above)*, a high school that prepared students for a teaching career. Only African American students attended this segregated school, which was built in the 1870s. Miss Lizzie Knowles *(inset)* was the principal at both the Navy Hill School and the Colored Normal School.

Even gathering for funerals of friends and loved ones would have been against the law. Secret societies formed in cities all over Virginia as slaves attempted to take care of one another. Members of the societies assisted the sick and the dying, buried the dead, and aided widows and orphans.

The secretary of these secret societies had to be able to read, write, and do math. The secretary collected payments from members, who slipped money into a hidden record book. When someone died, members had to apply for permits to attend the funeral. But it was still not safe for them to march from the church in a group. They had to wait until they were safely out of sight to form a line. After the Civil War, these secret groups came out of hiding and continued to help their members.

The society Maggie joined was named for the apostle Luke in the Bible's New Testament. He treated the sick. The original Order of St. Luke was an all-female organization in Great Britain. Two British women came to the United States to teach African American women its principles.

St. Luke spread from Maryland into Virginia. Later, most of the Virginia branches, or councils, broke away from the original Grand United Order of St. Luke. In Virginia, men were allowed to join and the name was changed to the Independent Order of St. Luke. Its purpose was to provide burial insurance and food and clothing for its needy members.

A group that provided people with burial insurance did not sound like a club a fourteen-year-old would want to join. But the Good Idea Council was like a scouting organization. Members earned badges for community services and moved up in rank. Meetings involved regalia, such as special sashes and hats, and complicated rituals such as a secret handshake.

Maggie had always loved theater of any kind. Parades, circuses, and marching bands had captured her attention since she was a little girl. She enjoyed the order of the meetings and followed rules and procedures to the letter. Maggie's mother also joined the Good Idea Council.

The Reverend Holmes and Deacon White had helped form the local Order of St. Luke, so the tie between church and community was further

The Reverend James Holmes *(left)* and Deacon William White *(right)* of the First African Baptist Church were among the founders of the Richmond Independent Order of St. Luke. The order was formed in the late 1800s.

strengthened in Maggie's mind. The motto of the Order of St. Luke was "Love, purity, and charity." It became Maggie's motto too. She visited the sick, helped bag groceries and clothing for the needy, and wrote encouraging notes to shut-ins (sick people).

When she was sixteen, Maggie was elected council secretary, a job she took seriously. She was also chosen to be a delegate at the council's annual convention in Petersburg, Virginia, in August of that year. Maggie's life was filled to the brim, with her office and duties in St. Luke, school, church, Sunday school, and chores at home.

She should have graduated from normal school in 1882. But in the fall of 1881, the Richmond school board added a language requirement. High school seniors could not graduate without a year of Latin, French, or German. Maggie's class had to stay an extra year. It was a hardship for many who were needed at home and who struggled to find money for clothes and books.

White public schools customarily held graduation exercises in the large, stately Richmond Theater. Normally African Americans had their graduation ceremonies in the First African Baptist Church, which seated up to two thousand. But the church decided to ban school ceremonies, political rallies, and feasts. It reserved the building for religious purposes only.

The principal, Miss Knowles, wrote to other black churches, asking if the normal school could use their facilities for graduation exercises. But Maggie's class insisted on holding its ceremony in the Richmond Theater.

The graduating class of 1883 had only ten students. Maggie achieved the highest grade point average. But others had performed well too, and many would go on to have illustrious careers. Maggie's childhood friend Wendell Dabney would become an editor for a newspaper in Ohio. Sarah Garland Jones became the first woman—not just African American woman—to practice medicine in Virginia. She also founded a hospital. Other classmates worked in law and education. The ten students met with the school superintendent, Miss Knowles, and the faculty of the normal school. Maggie persuaded Wendell to be the class spokesperson. Fiercely determined, the students decided to go on strike.

Wendell Dabney reported later, "We were determined not to go to any church. . . . The Richmond Theater or nowhere."

The school authorities told them if they didn't participate in graduation exercises, wherever they were held, they would not graduate at all. Maggie and the others looked at one another. All those years of hard work, down the drain. Without a diploma, they couldn't teach. Their families were counting on them to get good jobs, to ease financial struggles. Maggie and Wendell believed Miss Knowles was on their side. "Sorely was she afflicted by our stand," Dabney wrote. "But in her heart, she knew we were right."

The class held fast. Then some of the students began to waver, afraid they would not graduate.

Maggie and her classmates fought for the right to hold graduation ceremonies in the Richmond Theater *(above)*, traditionally
reserved for the graduations of all-white schools. Although the
students were finally allowed to use the facility, the theater's
management only permitted them to use the balcony.

Remembering Patrick Henry's famous stand in Saint
John's Church, Wendell rose up and shouted, "Our
parents pay taxes just the same as you white folks,
and you've got no business spending big money out
of those taxes to pay for the theater for white children
unless you do the same for the black children. We
won't go to any church, graduation or no graduation,"
he concluded, dropping into his chair. Nobody in
school had ever talked like that to the faculty before.
Impressed by Wendell's passion, the teachers and
staff backed down. Maggie's class won the battle!

But the Richmond Theater management said the
normal school must hold their exercises in the balcony, also called the peanut gallery. Only whites

could reserve the orchestra section. The class of 1883 stuck to their resolve, replying they wouldn't graduate in the Richmond Theater unless they were permitted to use the entire facility.

Maggie's class strike was getting attention in the newspapers. The June 23 issue of the *New York Globe* stated that "members of this class are already benefactors of their race. They have sent out the decree that they don't intend to be insulted."

Adding to Maggie's stress at this time, her biological father, Eccles Cuthbert, came back into her life. He bought her a new dress to wear to the ceremony. Elizabeth would not let Maggie have the dress. Maggie's mother may have been angry that Cuthbert was trying to get into her daughter's good graces after so many years. Whatever the reason, she threw the dress into the wood-burning stove. That was probably Maggie's last contact with her biological father.

Graduation exercises were not held in any church or at the Richmond Theater. Instead, the Class of 1883 met in the assembly room of the normal school. The room was too small for all the students' friends and family members, so only those who had tickets were admitted. Police officers stood at the doors to keep order.

Organ and cornet music accompanied Maggie's class march into the assembly room. The Reverend Holmes's son, John, gave the valedictorian's speech. Maggie's classmates read essays and recitations. One student, Caroline Hill, read her essay, "The True Teacher." The essay was reprinted in the *New York*

Globe. Miss Maggie Mitchell read "The Law of Death." The *Richmond Dispatch* and the *Globe* commented on many of her classmates' selections, but not Maggie's.

As a member of her distinguished graduating class, Maggie Lena Mitchell had bravely participated in the first black student strike ever. But she had yet to find her own voice.

Maggie Walker graduated from normal school in 1883, the year this photograph was taken.

CHAPTER FOUR

FROM MISS MAGGIE TO MRS. WALKER

In a studio portrait taken around the time of her graduation, Maggie Mitchell wore a long, slim-fitting black dress with a white collar. Her braided hair was piled high on her head. Frizzled bangs, the popular style of the day, softened her broad forehead. She gazed directly into the camera, as if looking into her future.

At sixteen Maggie was among the first well-educated African Americans in Richmond. Her diploma opened doors that had been closed to African Americans. Maggie would never have to take in laundry, as her mother did.

Life in Richmond's African American community was changing. Maggie was part of sweeping reforms that began before she was born. As a direct result of the Civil War, three amendments were ratified (passed and added) to the U.S. Constitution.

The Thirteenth Amendment, passed in 1866, had officially abolished slavery. Although African Americans were no longer slaves, they weren't full citizens, either. The Fourteenth Amendment had become law in 1868. It protected African Americans under the law and recognized them as citizens of the United States. As part of the Fourteenth Amendment, African American males had been granted the right to vote.

This amendment had been added to keep whites from denying African Americans the right to vote. It was rarely enforced, however, and many southern states found ways to get around the law.

In 1870 the Fifteenth Amendment gave males aged twenty-one and older, black and white, the right to vote. Some southern states reacted by requiring voters to pass a literacy test and pay a poll tax, a tax at the polling, or voting, place. Since former slaves hadn't been allowed to learn to read and write and since most had little money, they had difficulty meeting the requirements.

This illustration from the 1800s depicts African American male voters lining up at the polls in Richmond, Virginia, in 1871.

A collage displays the members in the Virginia House of Delegates in 1871. For the first time, African American delegates *(pictured in bottom row)* served in the state senate.

The Old South was gradually becoming the New South. For the first time in Virginia, blacks were elected to the Virginia House of Delegates (the state senate) and to Richmond's board of education. The Readjuster Party, a combination of black and white Republicans and white Democrats, controlled Virginia's politics. Readjusters promoted the Fifteenth Amendment and advanced black rights and interests.

African American citizens met at the First African Baptist Church to discuss racial politics and other problems facing them. One was the teacher situation. A. E. Randolph, a local African American attorney who had graduated from Yale University, argued that African American teachers should teach African American children. The Yankee schoolmarms and southern white teachers only saw their students in the classroom. African American teachers knew the needs of their pupils because they lived in the same community. They met their students' families on the streets and chatted with them in church.

If only white teachers were allowed to teach in their schools, Randolph pointed out, why train African Americans to be teachers? Where would they get a job? Why should the school board hire white teachers, he wondered, when there were qualified black teachers better suited to the job?

Later that year, the school board voted to appoint African American principals and teachers to all black schools. The normal school that Maggie attended was the only exception. Records don't state why, but the reason may have been because Miss Knowles was such an effective, trusted principal.

In the fall of 1883, Maggie Mitchell was one of twenty-two new African American teachers who were appointed to the city system. Miss Maggie Mitchell, as she was called, was hired to teach at the Valley School where she had been a student years before. James H. Hayes was her principal.

For a starting monthly salary of $35, Mitchell taught the second semester of first primary B (first grade) and the second semester of third grammar B (third grade). At the time, students were promoted every half year instead of every year. Mitchell was later given a raise to $42.50 a month when she taught third grammar A for a year. It was good money, better than her mother had ever earned. But if Mitchell became sick, she had to hire her own substitute at the rate of one dollar a day.

Mitchell loved teaching children to read and write, enabling them to "ride the wind anywhere." As much as she loved teaching, though, she wished she could have new books and furnishings in her classrooms. Valley School was as run down as it had been when she was a student there. Mitchell wrote lessons on a cracked blackboard and passed out tattered textbooks. Blacks had won the right to have all-black faculty in their schools. But funding for improvements still went to the white schools.

The gains African Americans had forged in the education community were only temporary. In the spring of 1884, the reign of the Readjuster Party ended. All African American principals and male teachers were fired. Maggie Mitchell taught her third year at Valley School under a white principal.

Though her mother had been a laundress, Mitchell's education and position as a teacher made her a professional. She was accepted into Richmond's black upper-class community. Mitchell joined the Acme Literary Society. The group was formed to "hold discussions, lectures, and to consider questions of vital importance to our people." James Hayes, Mitchell's former Valley School principal, was president. The group elected Mitchell to be its fifth vice president. Members read papers on business and race issues, such as "Our Colored Businessman" and "The Relative Condition of the Colored Man North and South." They also presented musical performances and recitations. Mitchell met influential activists such as Rosa Dixon Bowser, Richmond's first African American woman teacher, and R. T. Hill, a businessman and publisher.

Teaching at the Valley School and at Sunday school and working for St. Luke and the literary society kept Mitchell busy. But she still found time to socialize. A popular gathering place for young people was on the steps on the Marshall Street side of the First African Baptist Church. That was where Maggie Mitchell met Armstead Walker.

Handsome Armstead Walker was one of Richmond's most eligible bachelors. Fifteen years older than Mitchell, Walker had graduated from the African American normal school in 1875. His father owned a brick contracting business and had built many homes in the city. The Walker family was well respected.

Maggie and Armstead had much in common—they both wanted good, successful lives. They fell in love, and on September 14, 1886, Maggie and Armstead were married by the Reverend Holmes in the First African Baptist Church.

The newlyweds lived with Armstead's parents at 912 North Seventh Street for a while. But by 1888, they moved to their own house on 719 North Third Street. Under Virginia law, married women could not teach, but Maggie Walker refused to spend her days as a housewife or become involved in the social whirl.

Maggie *(left)*, pictured here around 1885, married Armstead Walker *(right, photo dated 1905)* in 1886. The Reverend Holmes of the First African Baptist Church, who had married Maggie's mother and stepfather many years earlier, presided over the service.

"A woman's activities should no more be circumscribed [narrowed] to domestic duties, regardless of her inherited gifts and inclinations, than it is sensible to say every man should be a merchant," she wrote later. "Let woman choose her own vocation."

Maggie Walker took accounting and business classes at night. These were offered to whites in high school, but not to blacks. She continued to teach Sunday school and participated in conferences run by the Virginia Educational and Historical Association. Even though she was no longer teaching, the meetings provided an opportunity to discuss topics concerning the black community. Walker never lost sight of her personal goal to make the world a better place for African Americans.

Having a family was also important to her. On December 9, 1890, she gave birth to Russell Eccles Talmadge Walker. Though Maggie Walker had no dealings with her biological father, she gave his first name, Eccles, to her son. Eccles Cuthbert was still living and working as a news editor in Richmond as late as 1890, even though he disappeared entirely from Maggie Walker's life.

Her first baby's delivery was difficult, as Walker later recorded: "The little baby was placed on the hearth to die, so bruised was he." She wrote, "His birth was unnatural in that he had to be taken by Drs. Ross, Michaux, and Dismond. He was crushed and bruised about the face and head. . . . I was ill but happy. I was so anxious for a little baby—to love, to rear, to follow by day and night, to see develop into a great and useful man."

The difficult birth almost killed Walker too. She was confined to bed for five months, but the skilled hands of excellent nurses brought both her and Russell back to good health.

Three years later, on July 8, 1893, Walker had another son. The baby, named Armstead Mitchell, lived only seven months. His death on February 4, 1894, filled the Walker household with sadness.

Another tragic event occurred in 1894. Maggie's brother Johnnie, who had been living in New York, came back to Richmond. Broke and ill with tuberculosis, Johnnie moved in with the Walkers. She nursed him and took care of him as she had when they were children. But Johnnie died of his disease on April 24, 1894. Though he left behind no family dependent on his support, Johnnie Mitchell died as his father had, without savings or insurance.

The deaths of two loved ones within two months were almost too much for Walker to bear. Her husband brought his niece to live with them. Margaret Anderson, or Polly, as she was called, was his sister's child, but she had been living with her grandparents. The Walkers adopted Polly. She helped with household chores, and she also cared for Russell.

Later in 1894, the Walkers moved from Third Street to 907 North Seventh Street, to a house across the street from Armstead's parents. A third son, Melvin DeWitt Walker, was born there on August 10, 1897.

Walker recovered quickly from Melvin's birth, eager to throw herself into work again. In addition to her church duties and position at St. Luke's, she joined and became secretary of the Ladies' Auxiliary of the Richmond Patriarchie of the Odd Fellows, one of her husband's fraternal organizations.

But activities such as putting on five-day Easter fund-raisers were not fulfilling enough. Walker wanted to do something more important with her time. She longed to make a real contribution to her community.

CHAPTER FIVE

SERVING THE COMMUNITY

Walker moved steadily up through the ranks of the Order of St. Luke. As one of the council's unpaid officers, she went from Right Worthy Grand (RWG) outside sentinel to RWG vice chief. In 1890 she became the Right Worthy Grand Chief, the highest volunteer office within the organization. She continued to be a representative to the annual convention in August. Fewer than 10 percent of the members were appointed delegates to the annual convention. Walker had been one since she was a teenager still in normal school.

Fraternal organizations such as the Order of St. Luke were the heartbeat of Richmond's African American community. Other groups, including the Odd Fellows, Prince Hall Masons, Knights of Pythias, and the Grand United Order of the True Reformers, competed aggressively with St. Luke for members.

The strongest and most established group appeared to be the True Reformers. This fraternal organization began gaining strength during Walker's high school years. The True Reformers was organized by a former slave, William Washington Browne.

W. W. Browne envisioned a large corporation that would do more for blacks than a simple mutual aid society such as the Order of St. Luke. Browne dreamed of black-owned businesses and greater opportunities for employment beyond the usual shoeshine stands, domestic jobs, and social services. He saw a fraternal organization that would be a self-supporting community. Browne also believed women should be included at all levels in the organization.

Walking around the streets of Richmond in his long black clergyman's coat, Browne gave people the impression he was an eccentric instead of a great visionary. But he had many workable ideas, as Walker later acknowledged:

> Here comes a man with a pencil in his hand and a scheme in his head [for] an insurance association and a banking house.
>
> When Reverend W.W. Brown came to us years ago, with his ever inseparable bundle of papers covered with figures . . . he was working out an evolving process by which the dollars and cents of the race could be employed for their own financial benefits and uplift. He was a long ways ahead of the rank and file of his associates; so far ahead they could not see him.

From the mid-1880s to the mid-1890s, the True Reformers organization blossomed with an insurance division, a children's savings plan called the Rosebud Division, a weekly newspaper, a real estate agency,

A former slave, William Washington Browne (1849–1897) founded the Order of the True Reformers in 1881. Walker wanted to bring many of Browne's innovative ideas into the Order of St. Luke.

and the first African American bank charter. With members' dues coming into the organization every month, Browne had enough funds to open the bank in his home in 1889.

While the True Reformers strode confidently forward with their dazzling plans, Walker's organization seemed pale in comparison. Though St. Luke didn't receive as much publicity, in 1885 they actually had more dues-paying members—2,328 St. Luke members compared to 2,000 Reformers. In that year, the True Reformers started their juvenile savings division. At the St. Luke annual convention, which Walker attended, the group voted down a similar program.

Walker had already devoted years to the Order of St. Luke. She wanted to help make St. Luke more competitive. At meetings she brought up some of Browne's innovative ideas, such as starting their own bank. But everyone thought those suggestions were too risky.

With so many fraternal organizations competing for members, St. Luke needed an organizing deputy, or recruiter. In 1891 Maggie Walker became St. Luke's leading recruiter. Instead of simply encouraging friends or church acquaintances, she traveled all over Virginia to recruit new members. Thirty new members could create a new branch council. Maggie presided over the initiation ceremonies, flawlessly performing the elaborate rituals.

In 1895, at the annual convention in Norfolk, Virginia, the speaker the Reverend Z. D. Lewis encouraged women in the organization to develop a juvenile department of St. Luke. Walker had been waiting for this opportunity. At last, the group had a way to help the children of the community. She believed children should reach for the stars and hold high ideals. "Our hope for the future lies with the children," she wrote later, "the youth of our race." What better way to instill St. Luke's core beliefs of love, purity, and charity than through a children's division?

So the juvenile branch of the Order of St. Luke was born. During the same convention, Walker and her committee worked quickly to set up the rules and regulations. Children aged two to sixteen were eligible to join the juvenile division. It was broken

Walker stands behind a group of neighborhood children in front of the St. Luke building in Richmond. She served as grand matron of the juvenile branch of the Order of St. Luke. This photograph appeared in the 1917 Fiftieth Anniversary Golden Jubilee Historical Report of the Order of St. Luke.

into smaller circles, usually named after flowers. This was undoubtedly Walker's touch. She loved flowers. As grand deputy matron, Maggie organized the first circle of one hundred children, called Violet Circle #2 (#1 was reserved for the grand matron, Ada Lewis). New members paid an entry fee of seventy-five cents—twenty-five cents was kept by the recruiting member—and ten cents in dues per month.

When Walker was elected grand matron, the position that headed the juvenile branch, she chose as its motto, "As the twig is bent, the tree is inclined." With its ties to the church, the group adopted the quote from the Bible where Jesus says, "Suffer little children to come unto me." In her bedroom, Walker had a popular print of Jesus with a group of children. Members of the juvenile branch were taught the meanings of both quotes.

As a teacher, Walker knew children learned best by having fun. She and her committee members organized pageants, talent shows, storytelling sessions, and parades. Bazaars were held at the St. Luke building. While the children were being entertained, they were also learning good health practices, to save money, serve their community, develop good manners, and gain the most from their education. Walker offered children prizes for attending all the meetings from September through July.

Every year around Thanksgiving, the group held

This photo collage was printed in the Fiftieth Anniversary Golden Jubilee Historical Report of the Order of St. Luke in 1917. It pictures all of the grand officers who presided over the Juvenile Department surrounding an image of Jesus Christ with children. Maggie Walker is shown at the bottom of the collage above the juvenile branch motto she chose.

"As the Twig is bent–the Tree is inclined"

a Sunshine Day. The juvenile department members were asked to "send out a ray of sunshine" by visiting someone who was sick, running errands, mowing someone's grass, or helping out in someone's store.

Walker, who still loved marching bands and parades, organized an annual parade. The children looked forward to it. Members of the juvenile branch, dressed in their cadet (student) uniforms, marched through the neighborhoods. The children wore satin sashes displaying the badges they had earned that year.

Within a year, membership in the juvenile branch had swelled to more than one thousand children. RWG matron Maggie Walker took her responsibilities seriously. No matter how busy she was with other duties, her work with the juvenile branch of St. Luke was closest to her heart.

Walker also took a group of older girls under her wing to give them leadership training. She encouraged them to learn how to earn their own living. Maggie taught them bookkeeping, how to run a store, and other skills they could use in life. She was keenly aware that young women wanted to get married, so she tried to prepare them for the realities of cooking, sewing, and homemaking. "You may win a husband by beautiful eyes, but it takes skilled hands—trained hands—to keep that same husband after marriage," the always-practical Miss Maggie told young women.

On the thirtieth anniversary of the Order of St. Luke, in 1897, Walker wanted to show off her poised young women. At that time, females were discouraged from participating in parades, but Walker was determined. She gathered young women in the basement of the First African Baptist Church. When the men began to file into the sanctuary upstairs to plan the parade, Walker led her young women upstairs too. The young women claimed most of the seats, leaving the men to scramble for places to sit down. Then Walker got up and spoke eloquently about the contributions women make in society. She didn't have to say anything about their not being permitted in the parade. With her smart young women filling nearly two-thirds of the church, Maggie Walker had made a powerful statement.

Despite all Walker's hard work as a recruiter, the Order of St. Luke began to fail. Rival fraternal organizations competed for new members. By 1899 the number of St. Luke Virginia councils had dropped from more than one hundred to fifty-seven. Members in Walker's juvenile branch outnumbered members in the adult councils.

Walker knew this when she took the train in August to the annual convention in Hinton, West Virginia, that year. But she and the other delegates were unprepared for the bombshell that Grand Secretary William Forrester dropped. Forrester ran the day-to-day business of the order. His office was the only paid position within the organization.

In his address, the grand secretary explained why the order was in serious trouble. Members were not cooperating with the officers. People were not paying their dues. Many refused to participate any longer, because, they said, St. Luke was an old-fashioned organization. When members died, the order couldn't pay claims. The order had only $31.61 in the treasury. They owed $400 in bills. St. Luke, Forrester declared, was finished.

A stunned silence filled the room. Walker knew how important St. Luke was to the community. She remembered how her brother Johnnie and her stepfather had died without a cent. She remembered how hard it was for her mother to afford a decent funeral for her husband. People would always need burial insurance. Who would take care of the elderly, the sick, and others who could no longer work?

As a final blow, William Forrester resigned. The audience was shocked. No more so than Walker, especially when no man volunteered to take Forrester's place. Walker wondered, why not a woman?

At last, members began to speak. Walker's name was called—she had been nominated for the position! After a long discussion and a vote, new officers were elected. Maggie Lena Walker was now the RWG secretary-treasurer of the Order of St. Luke.

Walker was handed the order's accounting books in a ten-cent basket. The council voted to slash the secretary's annual salary from three hundred to one hundred dollars, because of their financial problems. Walker figured her income as executive officer would be eight dollars a month. Eight dollars for countless hours of work! And a great deal of work needed to be done.

More than ever, Walker felt blacks should run their own businesses. Not just for their own independence but because the racial climate of Richmond—and Virginia—had changed. The era of Reconstruction had given way to a new period. It was known as the Lost Cause, referring to the Confederate defeat in the Civil War. Confederate veterans of the Civil War gathered for reunions. Statues honoring Confederate regiments were erected on battlefields. It was a time of remembering the war—and life before the war—as ideal and romantic.

In 1890 the statue of Confederate general Robert E. Lee had been unveiled on Monument Avenue, a new, wide street in Richmond. Huge crowds attended the event, waving Confederate flags and bellowing the rebel yell. Babies and small children were lifted

This statue of Robert E. Lee on horseback was created by French sculptor Antonin Mercié in 1890. Many southerners continued to honor Confederate war heroes, who fought during the Civil War to maintain the institution of slavery in the South.

to touch the ropes that pulled the curtain. Pieces of those ropes were cherished as souvenirs.

John Mitchell was one of Walker's classmates from the normal school class of 1883 and was editor of the black newspaper, the *Richmond Planet*. He wrote that the statues and ceremonies showed that the whites "still cling to theories [of race] which were presumed to be buried for all eternity."

As defeated white southerners sought to rediscover their pre-Civil War heritage, their views became more racist. Blacks were no longer welcome in white-owned stores and other businesses. Like others in her community, Maggie Walker was disturbed by the growing trend. But Walker had a solution.

John Mitchell *(right)* was born in 1863. He attended the normal school with Walker and was appointed editor of the *Richmond Planet* in 1884. He remained a civil rights activist until his death in 1929.

CHAPTER SIX
NICKELS INTO DOLLARS

Walker rolled up her sleeves and got to work. She planned to rebuild the ailing finances and membership of the Order of St. Luke. Then, using the combined strength of money and manpower, she would create businesses. Walker strongly believed in "buying black." Blacks doing business with other blacks spelled independence in Walker's book. "And here we are," Walker said in a St. Luke address, "shut out from employment in the concerns which we so largely support, by a prejudice higher than the Washington Monument."

Over the years, Walker had developed an energetic speaking style. Her piercing black eyes made each person in the audience feel she was talking directly to him or her. Her written speeches were designed to get the audience on their feet, ready to take her words to heart and act on them.

As grand secretary, she used her speaking talents before audiences in councils around Virginia, as well as Maryland, New Jersey, and New York. But not everyone reacted positively to Walker. In the early days as grand secretary, a woman in a leadership post was often greeted with criticism, usually from men.

"My position was one of a very awkward nature," she wrote later. "I traveled nights and days through the heat and cold sometimes meeting smiling faces but more often frowns and public opposition. I begged. I *persuaded*."

Gradually people began to respond positively. Drawn to the strong woman with the mellow, yet compelling voice, more and more members joined the Order of St. Luke.

Walker urged everyone to become involved—men and women in working-class jobs and professionals, such as doctors, lawyers, and business owners. They listened. They pitched in and worked on committees and brought in their own new recruits.

Within two years of Walker's becoming grand secretary, St. Luke's membership mushroomed to forty-five hundred. At the annual convention that year, Walker was given a salary increase. She had traveled relentlessly, often in rural areas, over bumpy, winding roads, in all weather and seasons. The board realized that Maggie Lena Walker was the person who had turned St. Luke around. She deserved the raise.

Walker was deeply committed to her role in St. Luke. Her position would enable her to best serve the advancement of African Americans.

As the new century dawned, white-owned businesses and factories flourished in Richmond. Though thirty-five years had passed since the end of the war, many white southerners were still finding defeat hard to swallow. Restrictions grew on black members of the community. It was the rise of yet another form of racial oppression called Jim Crow.

Jim Crow was the name of a character in minstrel shows—a popular form of entertainment in the nineteenth century. White men would paint their faces black to portray African Americans. They danced and sang songs, such as this one: "Wheel about, turn about, dance just so. Every time I wheel about I shout Jim Crow!"

A law in Louisiana dictated separate railroad cars for whites and blacks. Homer Plessy, a black man, was arrested for sitting in the white section of the train. In 1896 Plessy appealed to the U.S. Supreme Court, but he lost his case. News of the Supreme Court ruling that it was legal to have "separate but equal" accommodations spread like wildfire all over the South.

A newspaper headline from 1896 announces that the *Plessy v. Ferguson* case, which sought to overturn a system of racial segregation, was upheld by the U.S. Supreme Court. The ruling legalized "separate but equal" treatment for blacks and whites.

JIM CROW LAW.

UPHELD BY THE UNITED STATES SUPREME COURT.

Statute Within the Competency of the Louisiana Legislature and Railroads—Must Furnish Separate Cars for Whites and Blacks.

Washington, May 18.—The Supreme Court today in an opinion read by Justice Brown, sustained the constitutionality of the law in Louisiana requiring the railroads of that State to provide separate cars for white and colored passengers. There was no interstate. commerce feature in the case for the railroad upon which the incident occurred giving rise to case—Plessey vs. Ferguson—East Louisiana railroad. was and is operated wholly within the State, to the laws of Congress of many of the States. The

Besides separate-but-equal railroad cars, the South had separate water fountains, separate bathroom facilities, and separate hotel floors. All were usually far from equal. Signs that read "Whites Only" sprouted all over Richmond and other southern cities. African Americans were still struggling to find their place in the United States.

Life was not equal even in war. Walker defended the black soldiers who fought during the Spanish-American War of 1898. "[T]he brave black men, who gave up their blood and their lives . . . to save white men, have been forgotten," she wrote. "No promotions, no honor from this mighty government, only little mean medals while white men . . . are promoted and honored all along the line."

In 1902 the *Negro Advocate* newspaper praised Maggie Walker for urging blacks to stand up for their rights. "The audience was perfectly silent as she took the floor," the newspaper reported. "For fifteen minutes or more . . . she called upon the black men of Virginia to stand up for their rights, to fight slavery, to live for their children and for hers, caused old men and young to weep. It was a sight most unusual—a woman talking and men crying."

Walker also had plenty to say about a 1904 Virginia law regarding transportation: "Let us examine what is going on here, right under our noses in Richmond city in the Capitol Square. . . . The Negro in traveling pays first class price, for second and third class accommodation. . . . *Somebody must speak!*"

As blacks were also discouraged from buying

Walker is pictured here with her two sons, Russell *(left)* and Melvin *(right)* in this undated photo. Walker strived most of her life to help make life better for future generations of African Americans in post–Civil War America.

goods from white-owned stores and banned from eating in white-owned restaurants, Walker urged African Americans to open their own businesses. "To stand still in the same old rut would be a positive crime," she told them. "Why can't this great Order start and operate a millinery [hat] store and a factory for the making of clothing. We have the means and the brains. I am consumed with the desire to hear the whistle on our factory. Make no small plans. Small plans have no magic to stir people's blood. Let us be strong and make *big* plans."

Walker's big plans included having an office building. The three-story St. Luke Hall was constructed in 1903. (Later the offices moved to a four-story brick building at 900 Saint James Street.) To help the organization regain a financial foothold, Walker asked the board members to enforce membership in the insurance plan and to double the dues. St. Luke set up a college loan fund to give financial aid to deserving students.

"What we need is . . . a newspaper to herald and proclaim the work of our Order," Walker had remarked at the 1901 annual St. Luke convention, where she outlined her boldest plans. "No business, no enterprise, which has to deal with the public can be pushed successfully without a newspaper." The order began publishing a newspaper called the *St. Luke Herald*. The weekly *Herald* informed members what was going on within the order. It also became a platform for (a way to talk about) issues on unfairness to their race. The first editorial spoke out on injustice, mob rule, and Jim Crow. The newspaper included a section that published stories, articles, and poems written by children.

But Walker had an even bigger dream. At the same St. Luke convention, she also announced the need for a savings bank, run by the members of the order. "Let us put our moneys together," she told them. "Shall we longer continue to bury our talent, wrapped in a napkin and hidden away, when it ought to be gaining us still other talents?"

Two African American banks had been founded in Richmond by this time: the bank started by the True Reformers and the Nickel Savings Bank, begun in 1896 by physician Richard F. Tancil. Both banks operated out of their founders' homes. Walker believed the St. Luke bank would be larger and more powerful. "Let us have a bank that will take the nickels and turn them into dollars," she said.

Walker asked John P. Branch, the elderly white president of the Merchant's National Bank, if she could study banking at his institution. For three months in early 1903, Maggie spent two hours a day learning the general operations.

It cost fifty thousand dollars to get a banking charter (a legal contract). Walker directed the sale of fifty thousand dollars worth of stock in the bank to people willing to invest in a black-owned bank. This was no small achievement for a woman. The charter for the St. Luke Penny Savings Bank was granted on July 28, 1903. The executive committee of the Right Worthy Grand Council was named to be the bank's board of directors.

Maggie Lena Walker became the first woman bank president in the United States. She knew her unique position would work to the bank's advantage. She traveled up and down the East Coast to make speeches and urge councils to make deposits when the bank opened. "Bring it all back home," was the motto adopted by St. Luke Penny Savings Bank. Walker began signing her bank correspondence, "Yours for the uplift of the race."

Although Walker wanted to have women to run her bank, she made the wise decision of hiring Emmett C. Burke as cashier. Burke had been a bookkeeper for ten years at the True Reformers Bank. Women held seats on the bank board, and Mary Dawson became assistant cashier.

On November 2, 1903, St. Luke Penny Savings Bank at 900 St. James Street opened its doors. Walker knew an event of such historic importance deserved a grand celebration. Bands played spirited music, choirs sang, and people made rousing speeches all day. Walker prepared comments for reporters from the *Richmond News-Leader* and other newspapers.

She optimistically predicted the first day's deposits would total seventy-five thousand dollars. In truth, the receipts added up to a little over nine thousand. But the actual figures could not lessen the success of

This building on St. James Street originally was built for the Order of St. Luke. Walker opened her St. Luke Penny Savings Bank here in 1903. She was the first woman bank president in the United States.

the day. People from as far away as New York came to open accounts in Walker's bank. Customers streamed in and out of the building until eleven o'clock that night.

Walker worked tirelessly to promote her bank. She knew it was a big step for African Americans to put their savings into an institution. Most kept their money under the mattress, in a shoe box, or buried in the backyard.

"How many of you are depositors in any one of the four Negro banks in our city?" she once asked a group of young people. "The wealthiest men of our town . . . didn't start their account with millions, thousands, or even hundreds. It was a dollar or two to which they constantly added."

She urged children to be thrifty. Children who opened accounts were given numbered, locked banks to take home. When the child had saved enough small change to add up to a dollar, he or she took the home bank to St. Luke Penny Savings Bank. The bank was unlocked and the money added to the child's account. Children could also open a Christmas fund. Each week they would deposit a penny or a nickel, and by Christmastime, they would have enough money to buy presents. Walker's bank grew and so did St. Luke's.

In 1910 Virginia passed a law requiring all banks to be inspected by the Virginia Corporation Commission for bank code violations. The True Reformers Bank, the oldest black-owned bank in Richmond, had its license suspended for having too much of its customers' money tied up in loans. The bank closed later that year.

St. Luke Penny Bank was also inspected but passed the audit (review) largely due to Walker's son Russell. Russell Walker had developed the bank's accounting system and kept accurate books. Maggie Walker worked long hours to keep the bank from failing.

Later in 1910, a law required that banks be separate from fraternal organizations. Since it no longer could be associated with the order, the bank had to find a new building. In 1911 St. Luke Penny Savings Bank moved into a new three-story building on First

The staff of the St. Luke Penny Savings Bank stands in front of the newly opened bank building in 1911. Cashier Emmett C. Burke stands second from left.

Walker *(far right)* stands behind a teller's window with Emmett Burke *(left)* and her son Russell *(center)* in the gleaming new bank interior.

and Marshall streets. Large first-floor windows were framed by stone arches. Brass grills covered the tellers' cages. Walker's office contained mahogany furniture.

Walker herself often stood at the corner entrance to greet customers, wearing an elegant dress and a gold cross on a long chain. She stood as strong and proud as the stone and brick structure she founded.

Walker poses for a studio portrait around the year 1900.

CHAPTER SEVEN
A FATAL SHOT

In the fall of 1904, Walker had bought a house at 110½ East Leigh Street, on Quality Row, Richmond's most fashionable African American neighborhood. The two-story home had been owned by a doctor. Doctors, dentists, and other professionals were the Walkers' new neighbors in Jackson Ward.

Walker knew she had become a role model for other African Americans. She was an example of what could be achieved and what success could buy. Maggie Lena Walker was a successful, confident woman. She carried herself proudly and dressed in stylish suits and hats. She almost always wore her heavy gold cross on a long gold chain.

Her new house was outfitted with the latest conveniences such as steam heat, electric lights, and a modern bathroom. The decor included floral wallpaper, gilt-framed mirrors, and mahogany furniture. Walker had always loved flowers. Fresh-cut blooms filled vases in every room.

The former owner of the house, Dr. Robert Emmett Jones, had added a two-story wing to be used as a patient waiting room and medical office. Walker turned the long, narrow first-floor waiting room into a library. Bookcases held the Harvard classics, bound

Walker bought a new house at 110½ East Leigh Street. The home, which would grow to contain twenty-five rooms, was photographed in the 1890s during its occupation by former owner, Dr. Robert Jones.

editions of famous speeches, and a well-worn copy of Shakespeare's plays, inscribed to Maggie Mitchell, February 1882. Her collection also included volumes such as *The Ambitious Woman in Business* and *A History of the American Negro*.

Spring was in full bloom in April 1905, when a new department store was ready to open on the north

side of East Broad Street. The location was important. Broad Street represented the invisible dividing
line between white businesses on the south side and
black-owned enterprises on the north side.

Walker planned the opening of the store, the St.
Luke Emporium, as she did everything—with careful
attention to detail and with determination. It hadn't
been easy. She had worked in secret for two years
to buy the property at 112 East Broad Street. When
white business owners found out what she was up
to, they tried to buy the building. One man privately
offered Walker ten thousand dollars in cash to give
up her plan. White store owners threatened local suppliers. They suggested that the suppliers would lose
their white business if they sold goods to Maggie
Walker's store.

Walker wasn't scared off. She went ahead with the
renovations to the three-story structure. In the shop
windows, wax mannequins modeled the latest fash-
ions from New York City. Hats as big as dishpans,
draped in organdy and laden with artificial fruit or
birds' feathers, were fashionably tipped over the mannequins' eyes. Since the store was to open the week
before Easter, the hats should fly off the shelves.

Walker knew a small thing such as having a place
to try on hats was important. In white-owned stores,
African American women either had to place a sheet
of wax paper between their hair and the hat or they
weren't allowed to try on hats at all.

And so, on that spring day in April 1905, the doors
of the St. Luke Emporium swung open. It was one of

Walker opened the St. Luke Emporium in 1905. She aimed to run a department store where African American customers were treated with respect and the dollars they spent would stay in the African American community. Walker hired many African American women as clerks, creating jobs for them. The employees of the St. Luke Emporium are pictured here *(right)*.

the first African American department stores in the country.

St. Luke Emporium was an impressive building. It had an elevator and a modern electric sign. In her continuing efforts to further women's careers, Walker hired mostly female staff. At the time, shops customarily hired male salesclerks. Walker had firm beliefs about the role of women in business. "Since Woman possesses the exact same kind of brain that Man has," she wrote, "there is no reason why a woman cannot engage in any business a man can and be just as successful. Let our cry be: Give the young Negro woman a chance in the race of life."

Within six years as the leader of St. Luke, Walker had turned the order around financially. Membership had grown an astonishing 1,200 percent. Councils flourished in twelve states and the District of Columbia, with thirty-eight full-time deputies who organized membership drives.

Walker often proudly told about the shoeshine man who worked outdoors, winter and summer, in good weather and bad, at the corner of Clay and Second streets. He couldn't afford to buy a building for his business or even rent space in one of the fine city hotels.

When he joined St. Luke, the shoeshine man learned how to save money until he had fifty dollars. Then Walker helped him rent a building with three chairs. Within seven years, the shoeshine man had purchased his own shop with twelve chairs. He also bought a house and furniture for his mother. His account in the St. Luke Penny Savings Bank never dropped below five hundred dollars. He was truly a success story!

In November 1905, Booker T. Washington wrote to Maggie Walker. Washington, a former slave, headed the all-black Tuskegee Institute in Alabama. He asked Walker to write about herself and the Independent Order of St. Luke for his new book, *The Negro in Business*. Soon everyone knew who Maggie Lena Walker was and what she had done.

Walker, who admired Washington, later asked him to be the main speaker at a St. Luke convention. Although he couldn't make it to the August convention,

Washington came to Richmond that November to address the Negro Organization Society. Walker chaired the committee that made the visit possible.

The year the St. Luke Penny Savings Bank opened, the order had presented Walker with a fine carriage and a pair of matched black horses. She had a brick stable built at her new home, had the sidewalk paved, and had the yard fenced with elegant wrought iron fencing. The Walker home reflected its owner's place in the community.

As Walker's extended family grew over the years, the house was expanded to twenty-five rooms. At one point, four generations lived together. Walker's mother, Elizabeth, joined them. Polly, Armstead's niece whom he and Maggie had adopted, stayed with the Walkers until she married Maurice Payne in 1911. Later, Russell, who married Hattie Frazier in 1912, moved in. Maggie Laura, Walker's first grandchild, was born in the house three and a half months early. The premature baby needed special care. The Richmond hospital had no room for a premature black infant, and there were few incubators in the city. But Walker obtained one and converted a room into a nursery for her granddaughter.

Except for a fall in 1908 that had left Walker with a fractured kneecap, she was in good health. Armstead Walker was a mail carrier. It was a prestigious job for an African American man because it was a federal appointment. Federal jobs in those days reflected the political climate. When Theodore Roosevelt's presidency ended, so did Armstead Walker's appointment.

Walker *(standing center)* is pictured with some of her family members with whom she shared her home on East Leigh Street. At left are Russell and his daughter Maggie Laura, Walker's mother, Elizabeth Mitchell, is seated, and Melvin and his son Armstead are at right.

Though he lost his position in 1910, he was still involved in the Walker Brothers Brick Contractors business.

Russell Walker was a manager in the bricklaying firm for a while. Later, he developed the accounting system for the St. Luke Penny Savings Bank and wrote new insurance policies to cover the special needs of the elderly. Walker's younger son, Melvin, was studying at Shaw University in North Carolina. The Walker family was doing well. But on one hot June evening in 1915, everything changed.

At midnight on June 19, Russell told Melvin, who was home from school, that he heard noises on the roof. Burglars had been seen prowling in their neighborhood. The Walkers were having their roof repaired, and the workman's ladder was propped against the back of the house. The police came but found nothing. Everyone was still nervous over the possibility of burglars. Russell decided to borrow a gun from one of his father's friends for protection. Though his mother disapproved, the gun was allowed to remain in the house.

The next evening, Maggie Walker and her mother were sitting on the front porch. Her husband came home from a funeral to change his clothes. Events happened quickly. Alexander James, a boy who lived across the street, ran over to report his mother had spotted a man on the Walkers' roof. Russell dashed inside, grabbed the pistol, and raced upstairs.

Walker heard a shot. Later, she would describe the following scene in her testimony.

Russell came running down the stairs. "I got him!" he cried.

"Got who?" Walker asked.

"The man, he's on the back porch," Russell said.

Walker limped upstairs to the second-floor porch— her knee was still troubling her. She saw a man lying on the floor. Even before she touched the body, she knew it was her husband. And she knew he was dead.

Walker screamed. When Russell realized he had shot his own father, he collapsed against the wall, sobbing. Walker called the neighbor behind them and asked Russell to go for Dr. Hughes. Later, Russell would be faulted for not calling the police.

"Dear God," Walker wrote later, "give me the strength to understand. . . . Grant me the strength to carry on." She was going to need all her strength to endure the next five months.

When homicide detectives arrived that Sunday night, they were immediately suspicious. The house was filled with uncountable people. Walker continued to scream from her bedroom. It was determined that Russell had crouched in the bathroom doorway and fired at the figure through the bamboo screen on the porch. Even though no evidence could be found pointing to murder, Russell was arrested. His mother freed him the next day on bail.

The shooting made the front page of both of Richmond's daily papers. Headlines shrieked, "The Killing of Armstead Walker." The *Richmond Times Dispatch* played up the fact that Maggie Walker was "one of the wealthiest and best known women in the State."

Suddenly Walker's productive life became entangled in scandal. Because there were no eyewitnesses to the shooting, people up and down Broad Street discussed whether the death was really accidental. Rumors flew. They gossiped that Russell drank and didn't always get along with his father. People even whispered that Maggie Walker had asked her son to kill his father so she could get the insurance money.

On June 23, at the coroner's inquest (hearing), Walker was questioned on the witness stand for an hour. She gave her testimony promptly and confidently. The coroner's jury came to an inconclusive decision. They noted the lack of any evidence that Russell had deliberately murdered his father.

The ordeal was far from over. The next hurdle was the police court hearing, which was postponed and rescheduled several times. When the hearing was finally held, the judge dismissed the case on the grounds of insufficient evidence.

But on July 26, the grand jury met, called witnesses, and charged Russell Walker with murder. The trial was scheduled for October 5, 1915.

CHAPTER EIGHT
RIDING THE WIND

Maggie Walker looked out over the sea of faces in the audience. Two thousand delegates had flocked to the 1915 St. Luke annual convention, held in Richmond. With her proud carriage and composed features, Walker gave the audience the impression she was the same strong Maggie Walker. Inside, she was unsure of herself.

Normally she had looked forward to the convention, but this year, Walker was tired and worried. Though Russell had been acquitted in two hearings, his upcoming trial for murder hung over her.

The trial was still months away, but Walker found she couldn't slip back into her old life. She felt she too was on trial. For the first time, her leadership in St. Luke was being questioned. In addition to the shocking death of her husband, 1915 had been a difficult year for St. Luke. Recruiters squabbled over territory, especially if more than one worked within the same community. Rival councils feuded with one another. When Maggie investigated these problems, members grumbled about one person ruling the order. Maggie's four-year term was over. If enough people voted against her, she would no longer be RWG secretary-treasurer.

Walker in her office in the St. Luke building, 1915

The room hummed with voices. Some delegates believed the secretary shouldn't maintain control over all the departments in St. Luke. They had suggested creating several departments, each with their own managers.

Walker put aside her worries and spoke to the delegation with her usual confidence. She instructed the members to help St. Luke continue to grow. More fraternal organizations were competing for the same memberships. Recruiting new members and making sure regular members did not drop out were vital to the health of the organization.

But Walker also reminded the delegates of her hard work in her address: "In 1899 a man or woman could not be found willing to take the organization that was said to be dying. I took it; I nursed it; I have suffered for it. I have given it the best I had—the most active years of my womanhood. I have given up health, home, children, all for this great and growing organization."

At the election of officers, delegates rallied around Maggie Walker. They unanimously elected her as RWG secretary-treasurer, a position she would hold for the next nineteen years.

Russell's trial was rescheduled for November 12. On that day, he pleaded not guilty to his father's murder. The courtroom was packed. "Was there anyone left in Jackson Ward?" the *Richmond Planet* reported. A new witness for the prosecution reported hearing a fight between Russell and Armstead on that Sunday. Russell's attorney ripped into the burglar story, pointing out that only a stupid thief would climb a hot tin roof in daylight where everyone could see him.

Walker and Russell both took the stand. Walker testified for three hours, maintaining her poise until the prosecutor's hammering cross-examination. She faltered a few times, answering, "I don't remember." Her face showed the strain of the last few months.

At ten o'clock that night, the court adjourned (took a break) until Monday. On Monday morning, the jury still had not reached a verdict. Maggie Walker looked the picture of dejection in her black dress, her head on her satchel (briefcase). She had unshakable faith in her God, but this was almost more than she could bear. Her husband was dead, her son was on trial for murder, and she was weary to the bone.

At last, the jury returned with the verdict. The foreman handed the paper to the clerk. His voice boomed out in the tense courtroom, "We, the jury, find the defendant not guilty."

The triumph was short-lived. The months of accusations and hearings had left Russell depressed. He sank into despair and alcoholism. Walker struggled to help her son during these troubled years.

Besides these worries and her many duties at St. Luke, Walker also belonged to other black organizations. She helped found the Richmond chapter of the Council of Colored Women, a member of the National Association of Colored Women's Clubs (NACWC). She was a charter (founding) member of the National Association for the Advancement of Colored People (NAACP), an organization that fights against discrimination and segregation. Walker con-

In Chicago, Illinois, mounted police escort an African American man during the Chicago race riot in July 1919. Racial tensions in the United States heated up when African American soldiers returned home from World War I and no longer wanted to live under segregation and discrimination in the United States.

sidered her election to the national board of directors of the NAACP her finest achievement.

During World War I (1914–1918), African American soldiers risked their lives to fight for the United States. When they returned from duty overseas in 1919, they had little tolerance for racism. The black veterans fought back. In the summer of 1919, race riots erupted throughout the nation. Seventy African Americans were killed. Many of these young men were lynched, hung from trees by angry white mobs.

After the 1919 riots, African Americans looked to their own history for symbols to instill black pride. For example, Walker and other women in the NACWC restored Cedar Hill, in Washington, D.C. This was the home of Frederick Douglass, the nineteenth-century African American leader. In 1922 Walker and the St. Luke delegates took the train to Washington for the opening ceremony. "We have made this historic place a hallowed spot," Walker wrote. "Here let our boys and girls gather and receive hope and inspiration like Douglass to fight and win!"

When women finally gained the right to vote in 1919, Maggie Walker wasted no time. November 2, 1920, was the first election in which women could vote, and in September of 1920, Walker registered and paid her first poll tax of $1.50. She went to city hall many times to ask for more clerks to register black women. In October the committee of presidential candidate Warren G. Harding invited Maggie Walker to Harding's home in Marion, Ohio. At Harding's home, Walker proudly stood in line with five thousand other women at Harding's reception.

As president of the Richmond Council of Colored Women, Walker raised funds to support institutions for young women. Janie Porter Barrett's school for girls was one of her favorite causes.

Barrett's school, the Virginia Industrial School for Colored Girls, was a 147-acre farm north of Richmond in rural Hanover County. Its students were troubled black girls who were runaways, unwed mothers, or former prisoners. Barrett taught her students practical skills and self-reliance. For years Walker provided the school's annual Christmas dinner for more than one hundred people. She also attended

Born in 1865, Janie Porter Barrett was a founding member and the first president of the Virginia State Federation of Colored Women's Clubs, to which the Council of Colored Women belonged. Funds raised by the federation eventually allowed Barrett to open the Industrial Home for Wayward Girls, a rehabilitation center for African American female juvenile delinquents. It opened in January 1915 with twenty-eight students.

the closing ceremonies whenever she could, bringing the girls small gifts such as soap or washcloths. She loved being with these girls, delighting in the girls' singing and in the bouquets presented to her.

She wrote about one such visit: "The dinner tables white with linen cloths, silver knives and forks, china, everything more beautiful than in most of our good homes—oh, it was just as simple, homelike and sweet as loving hands and hearts could prepare."

Walker also understood the need for women's rights. "The emancipation [freeing] of woman goes bravely on, and today the other women of the world, save ours, are fighting life's battle in every occupation," she wrote. "Poverty is a trap for women, and especially for our women; but the greatest trap is idleness, from choice, or that idleness which is enforced by inability to obtain employment. When I walk along the avenues of our city and I see our own girls employed in the household of the whites, my heart aches with pain."

Walker used her achievements to set an example for all blacks but especially African American women. The economy was booming. It was a time of prosperity. Walker encouraged black women to start their own business, no matter how small. "Have you ever stopped to think that a business of your own could bring you economic independence?" she asked them.

During these years, Russell stopped working steadily at St. Luke and began hopping from one odd job to another. His wife, Hattie, left him, taking their daughter, Maggie Laura, with her. Like his Uncle Johnnie, Russell developed tuberculosis. Eight years after shooting his father, Russell Walker died at the age of thirty-three.

With her husband and one son dead, Walker realized life was short. Although she had accomplished a great deal, more than ever, she felt the need to throw herself into her work. "I'm beginning the year with the determination to do more for others—to live for others," she vowed in a diary entry.

With all her involvement with black women, it was only natural that Maggie Walker became friends with another powerful African American woman, Mary McLeod Bethune. One of seventeen children, Bethune was born in 1875 in South Carolina. No one in her family could read. When a one-room school was started, only one person in Bethune's family could afford to go. She was chosen. Knowing the importance of education, Bethune later founded the Bethune-Cookman College in Daytona, Florida.

Education and equality for African Americans were also important issues to one of Walker's friends, Mary McLeod Bethune *(right)*.

Though groups such as the NAACP improved lives for blacks in cities, Bethune had seen firsthand that blacks in the rural South suffered the most. Women, she believed, were the key to changing their lives. Many small women's clubs were scattered throughout the South. Bethune encouraged those clubs to unite. In 1924 Mary McLeod Bethune was elected president of the NACWC.

When Bethune came to Richmond, she stayed with Walker. After one of her stressful years of work and health issues, Walker took a much-needed winter vacation as Mary Bethune's guest at the college in Daytona. At the same time, she attended a meeting about starting a national women's organization.

Walker relaxed on the Florida beach, marveled at being able to eat fresh vegetables in February, and attended basketball games and concerts. She wrote in her journal, "A warm home welcome was given us, we were then driven to our apartment and cozily housed, at 9 P.M. we were in bed, in Florida, amid growing palms and flowers, in a school the work of <u>one woman</u>, a credit to any race. Mary McLeod Bethune can <u>never die</u>."

While life was not perfect in the Jim Crow South, Walker rode the wind of success. She remodeled her house and bought a new Packard auto. Her neighborhood, Jackson Ward, was called the Harlem of the South.

Harlem, an African American neighborhood in New York City, became known as the black cultural capital of the nation in the 1920s. With new freedom, blacks living in this area expressed themselves in dance, poetry, music, and art.

Such writers as Langston Hughes, Countee Cullen, and Zora Neale Hurston wrote about the black experience. These were works for African Americans by African Americans. Whites and blacks crowded into new jazz clubs to hear the music of Duke Ellington and Cab Calloway. Walker's neighborhood was enjoying the same cultural growth.

The heart of Jackson Ward was Two Street, or the Deuce. Just off Broad Street and only a block from Walker's house, the Deuce was lined with beauty parlors, restaurants, hotels, theaters, and a skating rink. Walker enjoyed an evening out to see a performance at the Hippodrome or catch a movie at the Globe.

The Cotton Club—a famous jazz club in Harlem, New York—
advertises performances by Cab Calloway and Bill Robinson in
1923.

In her home, she entertained Harlem Renaissance
poets Cullen and Hughes. Musicians Ellington and
Calloway were invited to Walker's house. Sometimes
she and her family sat around the kitchen table, talking with the famous guest long into the night. Bill
"Bojangles" Robinson, a movie star and tap dancer
who appeared in many Shirley Temple movies,
was born in Jackson Ward. Walker came to know
Robinson and his wife when they joined St. Luke.

Walker had always loved New York City and enjoyed her trips there on St. Luke business. When her
business meetings were over, she would stroll down
the city's famous Fifth Avenue and window shop. She

decided to hold the annual St. Luke convention in New York City in August 1925. That year's convention was filled with high points, which she described in her diary as a "Hallelujah meeting."

Two moments stood out in Walker's mind. One was when her seven-year-old granddaughter, Maggie Laura, addressed the children's group. Clearly, Maggie Laura had inherited her grandmother's poise and delivery in speaking before a large audience.

The second event that particularly pleased Walker occurred when the mayor of New York City presented

Walker's granddaughter, Maggie Laura, is shown here in the 1920s wearing her Order of St. Luke Juvenile Department uniform.

her with a gold key to the city. At the ceremony, Mayor James J. Hylan said, "We believe that of one blood God created all nations to dwell upon this earth."

Walker replied that "the delegates were happy to hear, once in their lives, one white man say 'Out of one blood God created all men.'" Things were changing. Maybe not as fast as Maggie Walker would have liked. But African Americans—both men and women—were making progress.

CHAPTER NINE

"CARRY ON"

Walker strolled along the edge of the ocean, letting foam-laced waves curl around her ankles. Russell's daughter, Maggie Laura, and Melvin's children, Armstead and Mamie Evelyn, shrieked and splashed one another. Her grandchildren shouted to Miss Maggie, as they affectionately called their grandmother, to watch them swim.

Walker loved the beach and often went to Buckroe, a black-owned resort on the Chesapeake Bay near Hampton, Virginia. She relaxed by the water and enjoyed being with her grandchildren.

When she began traveling regularly, Walker tried to combine work with play, especially during the months of August and September. She loved music and kept a large collection of sheet music on the piano at home. The radio in her sitting room-office was tuned to Metropolitan Opera broadcasts.

Walker often stopped in Atlantic City, New Jersey, before and after her New York business, either for conventions, get-together with friends, or recreation. "The great and wonderful ocean," she scribbled in her diary. The rhythmic waves always soothed her soul.

She returned to her work refreshed, ready to tackle the mountains of work waiting for her. Fall usually

Walker often vacationed at the seaside resort of Buckroe *(above)*, one of the black-owned resorts in the Chesapeake Bay area.

passed quickly. Sometimes Walker took her grand-children to the Richmond Day Fair in October. Then came her favorite season—Christmas.

Walker bought presents for her grandchildren in shops along bustling Broad Street—bicycles, horns, and record players. She spent hours decorating the chil-dren's tree and placed a wreath on her husband's and son's graves at the family plot in Evergreen Cemetery. Maggie Walker gave generously to her friends and wrote long special letters to many others. On Christmas Day, she received dozens of presents and hundreds of cards. The doorbell on Leigh Street chimed like jingle bells as visitors called throughout the day.

Walker's contributions to the community did not go unrecognized. In June 1925, the Virginia Union

University presented her with an honorary master of science degree. Walker's journal entry reflected her excitement. "A Memorial Day for me!!!" she wrote. "To live all these years, to work unceasingly, to do the best every day, brought a reward, an honor little dreamed of."

But her "unceasing work" was taking its toll. For twenty years, she had traveled tens of thousands of miles, either by automobile or train, including Jim Crow segregated railroad cars whenever she made trips down South. When she recruited new members in rural areas where there were no hotels or inns, Walker sometimes stayed in private homes without running water or electricity.

In 1926 Walker wrote in her diary that she often felt tired. She noticed that her legs, particularly the left one, felt heavy, stiff, and numb. "So anxious about my limbs which seem to have given entirely away," she recorded on January 6, 1927.

She sought treatment at Hot Springs, Arkansas, and Memphis, Tennessee, where she had massages and healing baths. Finally, doctors fitted her with leg braces. The braces hurt, but she was able to keep walking for another year. Even then she tried to maintain her strong image. When photographed, she hid the braces by having a child pose in front of her.

No one knew what was wrong with her. One doctor diagnosed "rheumatic affliction." If she had arthritis, Walker never complained of swollen joints, the major symptom of that disease. She probably suffered from a form of diabetes, as well.

Walker *(left)* in Hot Springs, Arkansas, is pictured with a friend in a souvenir photograph.

Maggie's condition progressively worsened until she was forced to use a "rolling chair," or wheelchair. People thought she had had a stroke or that the kneecap she had fractured back in 1908 was acting up. Maggie Walker was a tall, heavy, big-boned woman. Her weight and size did not help her condition. Her doctors told her she would probably never walk again.

Although Walker may have had trouble walking, that would not slow her down. She installed an elevator in her house and built wheelchair ramps from the back porch to the garage. The back of her Packard was redesigned to accommodate her wheelchair. Within three months of the doctors' gloomy prediction, Maggie Lena Walker was attending church and board meetings. The *Richmond Planet* called her the Lame Lioness. Nothing was going to keep Miss Maggie down.

Walker, in her wheelchair, poses for a photo in her front parlor in 1928. Despite her health problems, she stayed committed to her work and community.

The United States during the 1920s was a time of prosperity. After the end of World War I, people bought real estate, cars, the new electric laborsaving appliances, and stocks. Playing the stock market was as popular as crossword puzzles, a new craze. But by the end of the twenties, the freewheeling spending was slowing down.

Walker was well aware of ripples in the economy. By 1928 the holdings of the St. Luke bank and the other two African American-owned banks in Richmond had been dropping for two years. Walker urged Second Street Bank and Commercial Bank and Trust to merge with the St. Luke bank. She believed the three banks would be stronger as one institution.

In October of 1929, the New York stock market crashed. Stockholders panicked and sold their stocks, taking huge losses. In a single day, October 29, known as Black Tuesday, people who had started the day rich ended it poor. Banks failed. The country was plunged into what was to become the Great Depression (1929–1942).

Banks all over the nation were closing their doors. Walker knew that the bank merger was the only way to prevent a similar downfall in their community. She pushed until the merger was completed in December. The new institution was called Consolidated Bank and Trust Company. Maggie Lena Walker was named chairman of the board.

Though Walker's bank remained strong during the early years of the Depression, she had other worries. Her son Melvin spent enormous sums of money, amassing huge debts that Maggie had to pay. Walker was forced to reduce the size of the *St. Luke Herald* from a twelve-page weekly newspaper to a monthly letter-size bulletin. She also had to cut St. Luke employees' salaries. She even had to borrow to meet the payroll.

Her health continued to be a problem. Walker found it more difficult to get around, even with the wheelchair. The sun porch that overlooked Leigh

Street became her favorite place. She filled it with green plants, blooming flowers, and an orange tree. She spent hours there, watching the everyday parade of cars, people, and children. Sometimes real parades detoured down Leigh Street, just so Miss Maggie could experience the sight.

Walker's condition grew worse. She developed gangrene, sometimes an outgrowth of diabetes, in which poor blood circulation can cause ulcers.

The Order of St. Luke declared October 1934 Maggie L. Walker Month. The order commissioned a bust of Maggie, sculpted by J. S. Collins. Hundreds of copies of the statue were sold. Testimonials flowed into Maggie's home, including one from Eleanor Roosevelt, wife of Franklin D. Roosevelt, who was the U.S. president at that time. "I cannot imagine anything more satisfying than a life of the kind of accomplishment you have had," the First Lady wrote. "I congratulate you."

On December 15, 1934, Walker slipped into a diabetic coma and died later that day. It is said she spoke one last time to her family and community: "Have faith, have hope, have courage, and carry on."

As was the custom, Walker's coffin was on view for the public in her parlor. Thousands of people—black and white—lined the streets and passed through Maggie Walker's home, paying their final respects. The offices of St. Luke and Walker's house were flooded with telegrams, calls, and letters of condolence. The entire community mourned the passing of a great women.

On the day of the funeral, African American schools in Richmond were closed for the afternoon. Black and white businesses flew their flags at half-mast and lampposts in Jackson Ward wore black drapery. Ten troops of Boy Scouts and children from St. Luke marched in drenching rain as an honor guard. At the First African Baptist Church, which was filled to capacity, hundreds stood outside in the downpour during the two-hour service. Besides family, friends, and coworkers, Walker's service was attended by the mayor, the editor of the *Richmond Times-Dispatch*, city dignitaries, and representatives from many organizations. Maggie Walker was buried at Evergreen Cemetery, with the St. Luke ritual performed to perfection. She would have approved.

Tributes to Walker continued over the years. The 1935 St. Luke convention honored the memory of their leader with a poignant reminder. Her empty wheelchair was rolled down the aisle of the hall, decorated with a banner proclaiming, "Carry On."

In Newport News, Virginia, and in Walker's native city of Richmond, streets were named after her. Her church commissioned and installed a stained glass window of her likeness. Perhaps most significant, Richmond built a half-million-dollar high school and named it after her. The Maggie L. Walker High School opened in 1938.

Maggie Walker's life was the best testimonial of all. When the slaves were freed, some people

Maggie Walker High School, Richmond, Va.

This tinted postcard shows the Maggie L. Walker High School. It opened in Richmond, Virginia, in the 1930s and was one of two schools in the area for African Americans. In 2001 a local magnet high school acquired and rennovated the building. It is known as the Maggie L. Walker Governor's School for Government and International Studies.

suggested that the entire race would die out, because they could not live on their own.

Walker was proof that the African American race would not die out but would survive and thrive. Born the daughter of a former slave who could not read or write, Walker struggled to make her mark. She fought against racism during the years of Reconstruction and Jim Crow. Being a woman made her work even harder.

In a 1909 speech to the Coronella Literary and Art Club in Richmond, Walker had revealed her concerns. She said, "Negro women, hemmed in, circumscribed [limited] with every imaginable obstacle in our way, blocked and held down by the fears and prejudices of the whites—ridiculed and sneered at by the intelligent blacks. Yet, young ladies, despite the obstacles which are in our path, don't you know that you are enjoying opportunity by far superior to those which your mother enjoyed?"

The little girl from the alley never stopped teaching and never stopped reaching. She rode the wind to places others only dreamed of.

TIMELINE

1865 or 1867 Maggie L. Walker is born.

1868 Elizabeth Draper marries William Mitchell.

1872 Maggie starts school.

1876 William Mitchell dies.

1878 Maggie joins the First African Baptist Church.

1881 Walker joins the Independent Order of St. Luke.

1883 Walker is elected council secretary of the Order of St. Luke.
She graduates from Colored Normal School and begins teaching.

1886 Walker marries Armstead Walker.

1890 Russell Walker is born.
Walker becomes Right Worthy Grand Chief of the Order of St. Luke.

1891 Walker becomes a recruiter for the Order of St. Luke.

1893 Armstead Mitchell is born.

1894 Armstead Mitchell dies.

1895 The Order of St. Luke begins a juvenile branch.
Walker is Deputy Grand Matron of the Juvenile Department.

1897 Melvin Walker is born.

1899 Walker is elected secretary-treasurer of the Order of St. Luke.

1901 Walker starts the *St. Luke Herald.*

1903 St. Luke Hall is constructed.
St. Luke Penny Savings Bank opens in the hall.
Maggie Walker becomes the first woman bank president in the United States.

1905 St. Luke Emporium opens.

1911 St. Luke Penny Savings Bank moves to new offices.

1912 Russell Walker marries Hattie Frazier.

1915 Russell shoots and kills his father, Armstead.
Russell goes on trial and is found not guilty.

1920 Maggie Walker votes in U.S. elections for the first time.

1923 Russell Walker dies.

1925 Walker receives an honorary degree from the Virginia Union University.
New York City mayor James J. Hylan presents Walker with the key to the city.

1926 Walker is fitted with leg braces.

1929 The stock market crashes, and the three black banks in Richmond merge to form Consolidated Bank and Trust Company.
Walker is named chairperson of the board of the Consolidated Bank and Trust Company.

1934 Maggie Walker dies on December 15.

SOURCE NOTES

15 *Our Inspiration: The Story of Maggie Lena Walker*, produced by John S. Allen (Richmond: Signature Communications, 1998).

17 Maggie L. Walker, "Nothing but Leaves," address to Cornella Literary Club, 1909, MLW Papers, Maggie L. Walker House, National Park Service, Richmond, VA.

18 Wendell P. Dabney, *Maggie L. Walker: Her Life and Deeds* (Cincinnati: Dabney Publishing Co., 1927), 28.

24–25 Maggie L. Walker, "The Sunday School," addresses, 1909, MLW Papers, Maggie L. Walker House, National Park Service, Richmond, VA.

25 Maggie L. Walker, "Reunion of Old Pupils," address to Methodist Church, 1906, MLW Papers, Maggie L. Walker House, National Park Service, Richmond, VA.

32 Gertrude Woodruff Marlowe, *A Right Worthy Grand Mission: Maggie Lena Walker and the Quest for Black Economic Empowerment* (Washington, DC: Howard University Press, 2003), 18–19.

32 Ibid.

33 Ibid.

42 Maggie L. Walker, "Woman in Business," address to Virginia Federation, 1912, MLW Papers, Maggie L. Walker House, National Park Service, Richmond, VA.

44 Maggie L. Walker, diary, December 9, 1925, MLW Papers, Maggie L. Walker House, National Park Service, Richmond, VA.

44 Ibid.

47 Marlowe, 35.

49 Maggie L. Walker, St. Luke 1895 Convention Council address, MLW Papers, Maggie L. Walker House, National Park Service, Richmond, VA.

52 Walker, "Nothing but Leaves."

57 Maggie L. Walker, "If Christ," addresses, 1909, MLW Papers, Maggie L. Walker House, National Park Service, Richmond, VA.

57–58 *Our Inspiration.*

60 Maggie L. Walker, "Introduction of Mary Church Terrell," 1899, MLW Papers, Maggie L. Walker House, National Park Service, Richmond, VA.

60 Marlowe, 86.

60 Maggie L. Walker, "Benaiah's Valour," address, 1906, MLW Papers, Maggie L. Walker House, National Park Service, Richmond, VA.

61 Maggie L. Walker, St. Luke 1901 Convention address, MLW Papers, Maggie L. Walker House, National Park Service, Richmond, VA.

62 Ibid.

62 Ibid.

63 Ibid.

65 Walker, "Nothing but Leaves."

72 *Our Inspiration*.

76 Marlowe, 145.

77 *Our Inspiration*.

81 Maggie L. Walker, St. Luke 1915 Convention address, MLW Papers, Maggie L. Walker House, National Park Service, Richmond, VA.

81 Marlowe, 157.

82 Ibid., 156.

82 Ibid., 57.

84 *Our Inspiration*.

85 Maggie L. Walker, diary, March 25, 1925, MLW Papers, Maggie L. Walker House, National Park Service, Richmond, VA.

85 Maggie L. Walker, "Traps for Women," addresses, 1909, MLW Papers, Maggie L. Walker House, National Park Service, Richmond, VA.

86 *Our Inspiration*.

86 Maggie L. Walker, diary, January 1, 1925, MLW Papers, Maggie L. Walker House, National Park Service, Richmond, VA.

88 Maggie L. Walker, diary, February 27, 1930, MLW Papers, Maggie L. Walker House, National Park Service, Richmond, VA.

91 James J. Hylan in *Our Inspiration*.

91 Maggie L. Walker, St. Luke 1925 Convention address, MLW Papers, Maggie L. Walker House, National Park Service, Richmond, VA.

92 Maggie L. Walker, diary, August 24, 1926, MLW Papers, Maggie L. Walker House, National Park Service, Richmond, VA.

94 Maggie L. Walker, diary, June 4, 1925, MLW Papers, Maggie L. Walker House, National Park Service, Richmond, VA.

94 Maggie L. Walker, diary, January 6, 1927, MLW Papers, Maggie L. Walker House, National Park Service, Richmond, VA.

98 *Our Inspiration*.

98 Marlowe, 251.

100–101 Walker, "Nothing but Leaves."

BIBLIOGRAPHY

Belsches, Elvatrice Parker. *Richmond Virginia: Black America Series*. Charleston, SC: Arcadia Publishing, 2002.

Branch, Muriel, and Dorothy Rice. *Miss Maggie*. Richmond: Marlborough House Publishing, 1984.

Brands, H. W. *The Reckless Decade*. New York: St. Martin's Press, 1995.

Chesson, Michael B. *Richmond after the War: 1865–1890*. Richmond: Virginia State Library, 1981.

Dabney, Virginus. *Richmond: The Story of a City*. Charlottesville: University Press of Virginia, 1976.

Dabney, Wendell P. *Maggie L. Walker and the International Order of St. Luke*. Cincinnati: Dabney Publishing Company, 1927.

———. *Maggie L. Walker: Her Life and Deeds*. Cincinnati: Dabney Publishing Co., 1927.

Dailey, Jane. *Before Jim Crow: The Politics of Race in Post-Emancipation Virginia*. Chapel Hill: University of North Carolina Press, 2000.

First Baptist Church. *Traveling On: First Baptist South Richmond: The 133-Year Journey after the Civil War 1865–1998, The Wells, Binga, Ransome, Jones Years*. Vol. 2. Heritage Preservation Commission, First Baptist Church, South Richmond, Winter 1999.

Fitzgerald, Ruth Coder. *A Different Story: A Black History of Fredericksburg, Stafford, and Spotsylvania, Virginia*. Fredericksburg, VA: Unicorn Press, 1979.

Furgurson, Ernest B. *Ashes of Glory: Richmond at War*. New York: Knopf, 1997.

Hakim, Joy. *Reconstruction and Reform*. New York: Oxford University Press, 1994.

———. *War, Peace, and All That Jazz*. New York: Oxford University Press, 1995.

Hale, Thomas F., and Louis H. Manarin. *Richmond: A Pictorial History from the Valentine Museum and Dementi Collections.* Richmond: Valentine Museum, 1974.

Lowe, Richard. *Republicans and Reconstruction in Virginia: 1856–1870.* Charlottesville: University Press of Virginia, 1991.

Marlowe, Gertrude Woodruff. *A Right Worthy Grand Mission: Maggie Lena Walker and the Quest for Black Economic Empowerment.* Washington, DC: Howard University Press, 2003.

National Park Service. *Maggie L. Walker Oral History Project: Interviews with Mr. Anthony J. Binga, Mrs. Maimie Evelyn Walker Crawford, Mrs. Bernetta Young Plummer, Dr. Maggie Laura Walker and Mr. Armstead Walker. February–October, 1981.* Vol. 2. Diann L. Jacox, Mid-Atlantic Regional Office, National Park Service, October 1986.

Rouse, Parke, Jr. *We Happy WASPS: Virginia in the Days of Jim Crow and Harry Byrd.* Richmond: Dietz Press, 1996.

Russell, Dick. *Black Genius and the American Experience.* New York: Carroll and Graf, 1998.

Ryan, David D. *Richmond Illustrated: Unusual Stories of a City.* Richmond: Dietz Press, 1993.

Sandford, James K., ed. *Richmond: Her Triumphs, Tragedies, and Growth.* Richmond: Metropolitan Richmond Chamber of Commerce, 1975.

Tyler-McGraw, Marie. *At the Falls: Richmond, Virginia, and Its People.* Chapel Hill: University of North Carolina Press, 1994.

Tyler-McGraw, Marie, and Gregg D. Kimball. *In Bondage and Freedom: Antebellum Black Life in Richmond, Virginia.* Richmond: Valentine Museum, 1998.

Valentine Museum. *Fifty Years in Richmond: A Photographic Review: 1898–1948.* Richmond: Valentine Museum, 1948.

Varon, Elizabeth R. *Southern Lady, Yankee Spy: The True Story of Elizabeth Van Lew, a Union Agent in the Heart of the Confederacy.* New York: Oxford University Press, 2003.

Videos

The Maggie L. Walker Story. Produced by ComTel Productions. Harper's Ferry, WV: National Park Service, Department of the Interior, 1991.

Our Inspiration: The Story of Maggie Lena Walker. Produced by John S. Allen. Richmond: Signature Communications, 1998.

Other Resources

Black History Museum and Cultural Center of Virginia tour. 00 Clay Street, Richmond, VA.

Maggie L. Walker House tour, 110½ Leigh Street, Richmond, VA. Owned and operated by the National Park Service.

MLW Papers. Maggie L. Walker House, National Park Service, Richmond, VA.

Suggs, Celia, National Park Services ranger. Interview. Maggie L. Walker National Historic Site, Richmond, VA. September 2002.

Valentine Museum tour. 1015 E. Clay Street, Richmond, VA.

FURTHER READING AND WEBSITES

Brill, Marlene Targ. *Marshall "Major" Taylor: World Champion Bicyclist, 1899–1901*. Minneapolis: Twenty-First Century Books, 2008.

Finlayson, Reggie. *We Shall Overcome: The History of the American Civil Rights Movement*. Minneapolis: Twenty-First Century Books, 2003.

Greene, Meg. *Into the Land of Freedom: African Americans in Reconstruction*. Minneapolis: Twenty-First Century Books, 2004.

Hart, Philip S. *Bessie Coleman*. Minneapolis: Lerner Publications Company, 2005.

Jones, Veda Boyd. *Jazz Age Poet: A Story about Langston Hughes*. Minneapolis: Millbrook Press, 2006.

Landau, Elaine. *Fleeing to Freedom on the Underground Railroad: The Courageous Slaves, Agents, and Conductors.* Minneapolis: Twenty-First Century Books, 2006.

Meltzer, Milton. *Mary McLeod Bethune: Voice of Black Hope.* New York: Viking Kestrel, 1987.

Welch, Catherine A. *Ida B. Wells-Barnett: Powerhouse with a Pen.* Minneapolis: Twenty-First Century Books, 2000.

Maggie L. Walker National Historic Site
http://www.nps.gov/malw/details.htm
This site contains a brief biography of Walker and information about her house, a National Historic Site.

Remembering Maggie Lena Walker: The Making of a Black Bank
http://www.findarticles.com/p/articles/mi_m1365/is_11_34/ai_n6181262
The banking website tells about Maggie Walker as a business woman and bank founder and president.

INDEX

ABOUT THE AUTHOR

Candice Ransom has written more than one hundred books for children, including *Finding Day's Bottom* (Carolrhoda Books, Inc., 2006) and *Seeing Sky-Blue Pink* (Carolrhoda Books, Inc., 2007). Ms. Ransom holds a Master of Fine Arts in writing for children and young adults from Vermont College. She lives in Fredericksburg, Virginia.

PHOTO ACKNOWLEDGMENTS

The images in this book are used with the permission of: Valentine Richmond History Center, pp. 2, 68; National Park Service, Maggie L. Walker National Historic Site, pp. 8, 10 (both), 12, 30 (both), 43 (both), 50, 51, 61, 64, 66, 67, 70, 72, 75, 80, 90, 95, 96, 100; Virginia Historical Society, Richmond, Virginia, pp. 9, 24, 39; Library of Congress, pp. 15 (LC-USZ62-117099), 16 (LC-USZ62-58316), 23 (LC-DIG-cwpb-02905); Photographer unknown, *Maggie L. Walker and the I. O. of Saint Luke: The Woman and Her Work,* Wendell P. Dabney, 1927, pp. 19, 28 (both), 36; The Granger Collection, New York, pp. 20, 59; Courtesy of Beveridge Collection, Valentine Richmond History Center, Image provided by The Library of Virginia, p. 33; © North Wind Picture Archives, p. 38; Schomburg Center for Research in Black Culture, The New York Public Library, Astor, Lenox and Tilden Foundations, pp. 48, 85; © Hank Walker/ Time & Life Pictures/Getty Images, p. 55; The Library of Virginia, p. 56; © Bettmann/CORBIS, p. 83; Florida State Archives, p. 87; © Frank Driggs Collection/Hulton Archive/Getty Images, p. 89; Courtesy of Hampton History Museum, Hampton, Va., Image provided by The Library of Virginia, p. 93.

Cover: National Park Service, Maggie L. Walker National Historic Site (both).